P9-CAD-743

To a Wonderful Father

To a
Wonderful
Father

♔

HALLMARK EDITIONS

PHOTOGRAPHS

Colour Library International, Cover; Phoebe Dunn, page 25; Richard
Fanolio, pages 5, 9, 21, 37; Maxine Jacobs and Jim Lipp, page 45; Jim
Lipp and Richard Fanolio, page 29; Jim Lipp, page 13; Ed Seivers, page
33; Jack Zehert, page 41.

Copyright © 1973 by Hallmark Cards, Inc.,
Kansas City, Missouri. All Rights Reserved.
Printed in the United States of America.
Library of Congress Catalog Card Number: 72-83192.
Standard Book Number: 87529-299-2.

To a Wonderful Father

"my daddy"

Sometimes,
fatherhood must seem
like a forgotten role.

A father seldom
wins any awards
or hears the praise
he really deserves.

I guess I'm
as guilty as anyone
on that score...

*...so, this comes
because I want to say
I love you...*

...I'm proud of you,
you're a wonderful father!

You've helped make
my world wider,
pointed my way
in new directions...

...encouraged explorations down new and different pathways.

You made
the growing-up years
an adventure...

a time of games,
laughter, learning,
a time of love.

You've always been
a thoughtful father...

...with a great concern
for the little things

that make others feel important.

You've always been
helpful when I needed you.
You listen with love...

...you're able
to tune in on
the same wavelength
with me...

and your
understanding of me
helps me
to understand myself.

You're a
lots-of-fun father.
Hope you know that!

You take the time
to enjoy life...

*and to share
the joys of others.*

You add merriment
to chores, and make
good times even better.

You've been
an inspiration, too.

You may not know it,
but it's true.

You give life
an added meaning
and make its challenges
not a series of problems
to be met, but a wealth
of opportunities to enjoy!

Most of all,
you're a loving father...

which means so much!

You overlook faults
and shortcomings,
even as you try
to help someone improve.

You share your heart

so that others'
deepest thoughts
and feelings
grow and flourish.

You've brought me
so much happiness,
taught me
the important lessons,
given me
joyful memories.

Without your love,
these words might come
much harder,

but because you're you,
they're easy.

What more
could I ask for
in a father
than what
you have been,
than what you are?